ISBN NO. 978-0-9936007-0-8

Shelly The Star-Gazer

Written and illustrated
by Zuzy Rocka

For Evva

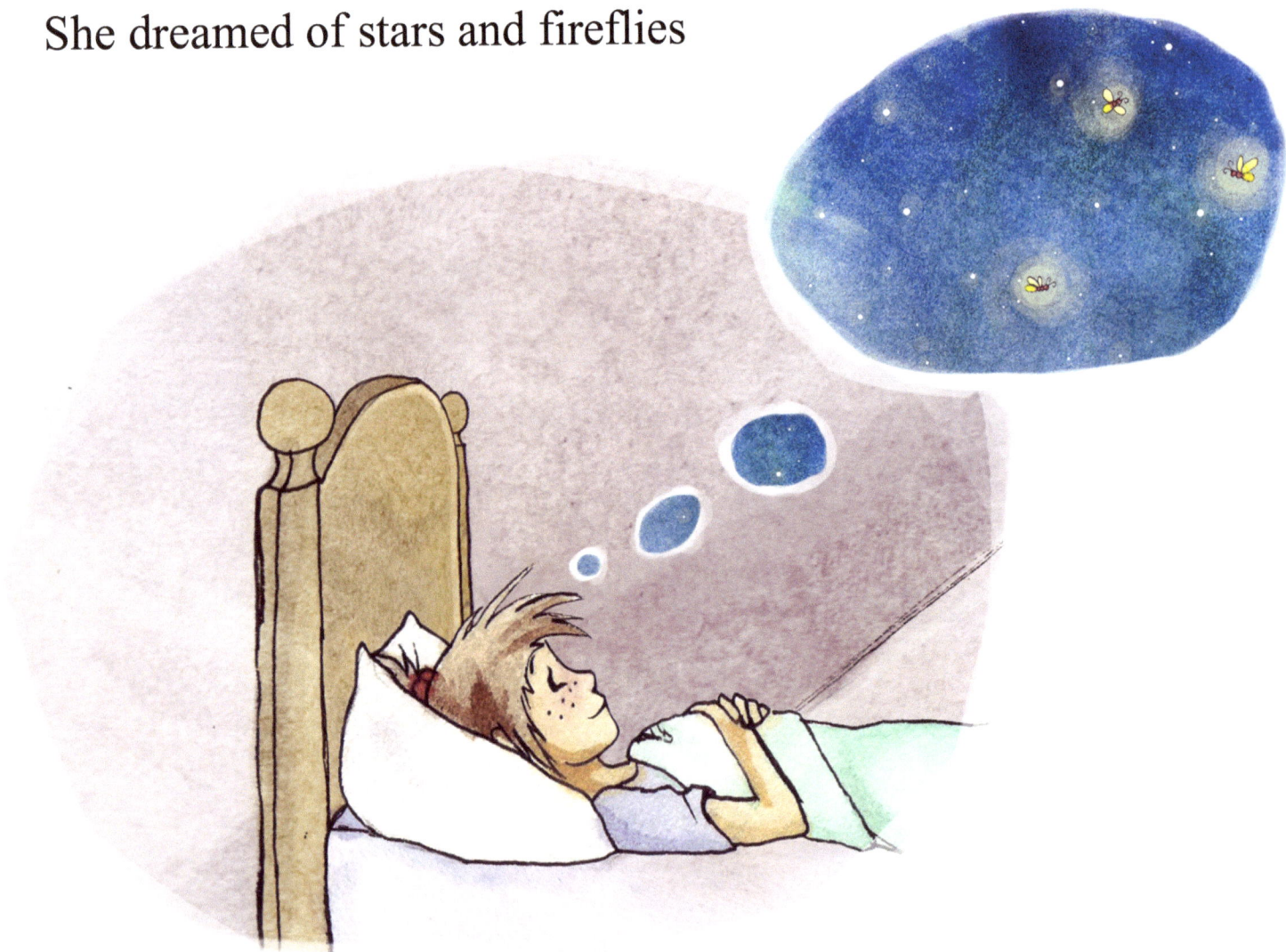

Shelly, Shelly, the star-gazer

Being in bed, didn't faze her

Every night she watched the skies

Looking up with widened eyes

She dreamed of stars and fireflies

One warm night, Shelly stayed up late

Sleepily watching, she did wait

For something different, something fun

About stars shining beyond the sun

She had already counted every single one

Shelly, Shelly, the star-gazer

Being in bed, didn't faze her

Just as she was about to take a nap

There was suddenly a loud "tap-tap"

Shelly yelped, "what was that?"

What could that sound possibly be?

She hopped from bed, to go and see

It was a shooting star from far away

"Come with us, come and play!"

Is what the little star did say

She climbed onto the little star

They flew up high!

They flew up far!

The clouds all grew and grew

And oh the stars!

And the sky so blue!

Shelly, Shelly, the star-gazer

Fireflies loved to race her

They flew about, as they pleased

Over rolling hills and whispering trees

Laughing through the warm night breeze

They raced and played, they had great fun

They all shared, and they all won

But then Shelly had to go to bed

To sleep and rest her little head

"I will see you again soon," Shelly said

Shelly blew a kiss and waved goodbye

To each and every firefly

Then the shooting star from far away

Took Shelly home, and he did say

"I am glad that you could come and play."

Shelly, Shelly, the star-gazer

Being in bed, didn't faze her

One night after Shelly watched the sky

She lay in bed, she shut her eyes

She dreamed of stars and fireflies

The end.

Hello! My name is Zuzy, how are you?

I hope you are good

and never blue

I'm from B.C. Canada, with lots to see

I love my dog Pepper

And big birch trees

I love bears and animals, of any kind

I love snow, the stars,

And I love to rhyme